BEHAVIOR SUPPORT STRATEGIES FOR EDUCATION PARAPROFESSIONALS

B Y

Will Henson, Psy.D.

ISBN: 1-4196-9612-2
ISBN-13: 9781419696121

Visit www.booksurge.com to order additional copies.

Also available at www.amazon.com

PREFACE

Some of the scenarios and events set forth in this book are based on or are composites of actual events. All names and potentially identifying information have been changed substantially in order to protect confidentiality. Any resemblance to actual events, locales or persons, living or dead, is entirely coincidental.

This book is intended to provide advice on handling disruptive behavior in an educational setting. It is sold with the understanding that the author and publisher are not engaged in rendering mental health or educational consultation or any other professional service in this book. The book should be used in conjunction with best practices and the law and its application overseen by qualified persons.

The author specifically disclaims any liability, loss, risk, injury, and educational or emotional impact, personal or otherwise, which is incurred as a consequence of implementing the contents of this book.

ACKNOWLEDGEMENTS

I would like to acknowledge all the people who helped me reach the point where this book was possible. I am indebted to all my colleagues I have worked with in schools, clinics and other facilities over the past years. There are too many of you to name, but you know who you are. I am grateful to all the teachers, administrators and paraprofessionals who have been encouraging in this process. I am also grateful mostly to all the young people I have worked with who have taught me, mostly through hard lessons, the best ways to serve them.

INTRODUCTION

One of the most difficult tasks faced by anyone who works in a school is learning how to handle challenging behaviors. A recent national survey of teachers found behavior intervention to be the area teachers felt *least prepared* for when entering the field. If teachers feel unprepared, you can imagine how someone without formal training might feel when tasked with handling a difficult behavior.

I believe educational paraprofessionals are some of the most important people in our schools. In fact, paraprofessionals are used for some very difficult tasks, and our schools could barely run without them. Schools pair them with students who exhibit disruptive behavior, utilize them as extra staff in rowdy classrooms, and use them to help manage hallways, buses, and playgrounds. They do all this tirelessly, often without any formal training. Paraprofessionals build important relationships with students and have an impact that is every bit as important as that of teachers.

This book was written specifically for education paraprofessionals. Paraprofessionals are known by different names in different districts. They might be called instructional assistants, educational assistants, classroom aids, paraeducators or education support professionals. This book may also be useful for bus drivers, food service workers, librarians, volunteers, and anyone else who sometimes needs strategies to prevent and address student behavior. For this reason, I will often use the term *staff member* in the text instead of a more specific title.   This book is also for teachers and administrators who hire, train, and supervise paraprofessionals.   This book is also intended as an introduction to behavior strategies for anyone who will work directly with students.

If you're reading this, it's likely you've already run across some problematic behaviors. Whether you come to this manual frustrated or hopeful, the important thing to understand is that changing disruptive behaviors *can be done with a high rate of success.* It is my hope that the information in this book will be useful to you immediately and will start making your job easier *today.* It is common for books on behavior to discuss theories and techniques yet leave out the important elements of what to say and what to do. Where possible, I have included examples of the exact actions you might take and words you might say in a variety of situations.

The term *behavior support* in the title of this book is important. The term educators once used was *behavior management.* Educators now use the term *behavior support* because we have found that our job isn't just to manage inappropriate behavior, but to find ways to foster and support the types of behaviors we want to see. Where I do use the term *behavior management* it is to discuss ways we prevent and react to behavior.

This book is your guide to handling behavior. I've taken some of the most important concepts in behavior and put them into a language and format that is easy to understand. This information comes from evidence-based practice literature and from many paraprofessionals, educators, and students I have worked with over the years. From them, I've borrowed what I know works.

A Note on Examples

Paraprofessionals work in wide range of classrooms with many different types of students in both special and regular education settings. Every example I give in this book will not work with every student. If you are a regular education staff member who works with a mainstream population, your response to a behavior may be very different than that of someone who works in a classroom for students with behavioral difficulties. There are some students with emotional and developmental disabilities for whom standard discipline doesn't work well. If you run across examples in which the suggested intervention seems too lax or too strict, remember that the examples can't cover every situation or student. The examples are there to give you ideas about how you might solve different types of problems.

TEAMWORK

Working on a Team

Paraprofessionals work as part of a team which often includes teachers, counselors, specialists, administrators and other paraprofessionals. Knowing everything in this book is much less useful than having everyone on your team become skilled in a few fundamentals and share common ideas, language, and strategies. More importantly, your team has to be planful; they must set up strategies that allow them to effectively prevent and respond to behaviors.

It is sometimes frustrating for paraprofessionals to begin the process of behavior planning because they are not the ones in charge of their teams. Teachers and administrators set classroom rules and policy; school psychologists and counselors are often involved with intervention planning. With so many people involved, it is vital that everyone act *together* on the information in this book.

Before you enter a new situation, find out what type of behavior system is already in place. If you are working in a teacher's classroom, it is important to ask a lot of questions about what your role will be.

Some Good Questions to Ask When Working in a Classroom

- What are the rules of your classroom?
- What have you found helpful in the past?
- What have you found to be unhelpful in the past?

- How would you like me to handle misbehavior?
- Would you like me take the initiative to handle behavior on my own, or would you rather address it first?
- How often should I check in with you?
- In what other ways can I help out?
- Are there students or situations I should pay extra attention to?

Inclusion and Mainstreaming Support

It is common for paraprofessionals to be used to accompany a single, high-needs student into classrooms to help that student access mainstream educational and social opportunities. In these situations it is important to make some decisions with the student and the classroom teacher regarding your role in the classroom.

- Will you work with that student *only* or will you help all the students?
- How obvious will it be that you are there for that student? Will you sit next to her the entire time, or intervene only when she needs it?
- How will the student signal you she needs help?

UNDERSTANDING BEHAVIOR

Why Do They Do It?

"Why do they do it?" This question has been asked for years by people who work with students who exhibit disruptive behaviors. Many answers have been suggested, from problems at home to lack of discipline to too much television. Why do students misbehave? Once we answer this question, deciding how to respond to behaviors becomes much easier.

"There is no bad behavior, just communication we do not yet understand." – Jaycee Bush

One idea about behavior is that students do whatever they want because they lack motivation, self-discipline, and effective consequences. Students have "figured out" that they can get away with misbehavior, or that they simply don't care. According to this idea, students *choose* their behavior, consciously weighing the outcomes and consequences. They decide they will curse at adults, skip class, annoy people, run down the halls, and refuse to do schoolwork because it is what they want to do and no one is going to stop them! According to this view, the best way to work with students is to find the right rewards and consequences in order to "motivate" them to behave properly.

A different view is that students' behavior is an attempt to meet an important need. This might include, for instance, a need to be successful, to be liked, to gain attention, to communicate something important, to be in control of a situation, or to avoid stress or failure; things all of us strive for every day. According to this view, misbehaving students do not "decide" to be *bad*. They are simply trying to meet important human needs in inappropriate ways. This view approaches student misbehavior as a deficit in the skills required to get needs met appropriately. When we view behavior this way, our job becomes that of educators, role models, and helpers, not disciplinarians.

Which view do you believe? Think about it this way: if a student is getting into conflicts every day with school staff because she feels unfairly treated (rightfully or not), are you going to get this student to give up her wish to be treated fairly for a granola bar and some free time on the computer? How about by taking away her recess? Would you give up being treated fairly at work for a ten-minute break and a cup of coffee? Hopefully not!

The Function of the Behavior

Before you decide how to respond to a behavior, it is important to figure out its **function** for the student: what is he or she trying to get, avoid, escape, or communicate by these actions? Once you understand what the behavior does for the student, you can help the student meet that need in another, more appropriate way. For instance, you may need to help the student find a new way to tell you (communicate) that she is feeling unfairly treated, and help her develop a sense of what is fair and what is not. I am not saying that we never give rewards or consequences; these have their place too. You can't, however, expect rewards and consequences to change behaviors when a student lacks the skills to meet his or her important needs below is a list of common functions of behaviors and sample behaviors you might see.

Some Common Functions of Behaviors	Sample Behavior
• Gain a sense of control	• Refusing to comply with a request.
• Gain attention and acceptance from peers	• Making inappropriate jokes in class
• Demonstrate competence or experience success	• Cheating at a board game
• Avoid difficult feelings (e.g. ,shame, embarrassment, anxiety, disappointment)	• Starting a conflict with another person to avoid the real issue
• Avoid frustrating or difficult work	• Refusing to do work
• Escape a difficult situation	• Skipping class
• Communicate an emotion (e.g., frustration, anger, or sadness)	• Yelling and cursing at a staff member
• Calm down when upset	• Acting aggressively toward an object
• Avoid boredom	• Flapping hands, fidgeting
• Avoid sensory overstimulation	• Pulling a coat over the head, hiding

One thing you may have noticed is that many of the sample "inappropriate" behaviors on the right can serve many functions. For example, a middle school student might skip class every day as a way to be with friends, to avoid confronting an embarrassing situation, to show the teacher he is mad at her or because he can't handle the noise level in the classroom.

I list these possible functions here because often times I see people who know only one function for bad behavior (usually it's "to get attention"). Every student who acts up then must want attention and the result is almost invariably to ignore or confront the behavior. Behaviors often have many functions, but the important part for educators is not just guessing the function, but helping the student develop the skills she lacks in the first place.

What else do you notice about these reasons for misbehavior? If you look at them, you will see they are all things we ourselves might want. No one wants to be frustrated, or sad, or embarrassed. And all of us want to be in control, to be liked, and to be successful. Notice that functions like "to make my instructional staff mad" or "to disrupt class" are not on this list (even though, it does seem like that is what some students would prefer to do). While we may see behaviors that have this effect, we can assume that underneath these behaviors are deeper, better-intentioned wishes for success, relationships, and happiness.

Replacing Behaviors and Teaching Skills

Now that you understand how a behavior can be an attempt to meet a legitimate need, you can see how students aren't going to be talked out of their favorite (and your least favorite) behaviors by rewards and consequences.

We began our discussion on behavior by proposing the idea that students' misbehavior is often due to a lack of skill rather than a purposeful choice. Creating a change in students isn't about teaching them how to behave. It is about teaching them how to get their needs met. What kinds of skills do students lack that might cause them to misbehave? There are important skills that students need to manage everyday life. As you work with students and see them trying to meet needs in inappropriate or ineffective ways, you may begin to realize which skills they are going to need in order to succeed in school socially, emotionally, and academically.

Some Important Skills for Students

- Self Advocacy: *e.g., choosing how to express frustration to a teacher who goes over material too fast*

- Problem Solving: *e.g., deciding how to handle a disagreement over the rules of a game*

- Planning & Organizing: *e.g., putting together a list of assignments and a timeline for how to do them*

- Socializing: *e.g., sharing interests with someone else*

- Managing Emotions: *e.g., being able to set fear of failure aside to try a math problem*

- Role Switching: *e.g., being able to put oneself in another's shoes*

- Cognitive Flexibility: *e.g. being able to accept a change in routine*

Brian

Brian was a student in a seventh-grade resource room. Brian was almost constantly making jokes and wisecracks during instruction. The teacher, classroom aides and I decided that the function of Brian's behavior was to get attention from his classmates and to be liked. We created an intervention with the team to reduce his excessive need for inappropriate attention. First, we changed his work group to put him with three other students we felt would be appropriate friends for him. We thought this would help him focus on individual interactions rather than trying to entertain the class. Next, we asked the paraprofessionals to give him a lot of attention in reading group for appropriate behaviors. Finally, each staff member made an effort to engage him before and after class and build a relationship with him. In about three weeks, we noticed he was not making nearly as many jokes during instruction. He now had plenty of attention from both his peers and from us. What's more, we came to like Brian much more when we took the time to get to know him.

Zach

I once had a first-grade student named Zach, who engaged in constant power struggles. If I ever asked Zach to do anything, his immediate answer was no. I decided Zach was trying to be powerful in the only way he knew how. Being the recess aide, I asked him one day if he would help me hand out the balls and recess equipment. Students had to line up and ask for what they wanted. It gave him a little bit of power. I also let him save out something for himself first. When he was done handing out the equipment, I told him what a great job he had done and asked him if he would help me the next day. I also asked him to come tell me quietly if he saw any students behaving unsafely on the playground or if anyone got hurt. When a new student transferred in that next week, I asked Zach to show him around the playground and explain the rules. I still had to blow my whistle at Zach now and then, but much less often, and when I did the response I got was much more pleasant.

Changing your Response

Disruptive behavior can trigger adults to act in predictable ways. When we view behaviors as willful acts rather than skill deficits, we tend to respond by demanding change, handing out consequences and engaging in battles. When we see students as lacking the ability to meet their needs we are free to respond differently. Often inappropriate behaviors continue because they serve a useful function for the student. Let's go over some examples of how a behavior might be unintentionally reinforced by well-meaning adults.

- A student disrupts class with inappropriate comments and jokes. Every time this happens one of the adults in the classroom engages in banter with him to stop. The behavior is reinforced by the adults, who give the student the attention he wants.

- A student often refuses to do what the teacher asks. She defiantly says, "No, you can't make me!" when the teacher gives her an assignment. The teacher often gets angry and argues with her, demanding she do the work. The student refuses. The teacher says she will get an F if she doesn't do the work. The student screams back, "I don't care." This student, who lacks the skills to advocate for herself in more appropriate ways, finds success by picking a battle with the teacher that the teacher can't possibly win.

- A student with a reading disability will do anything to avoid the embarrassment and frustration caused by a reading assignment. He throws his book on the floor when asked to read. The teacher addresses the behavior by sending him to time-out, and the reading assignment is forgotten. Time-out is much preferred by the student to embarrassment. The student is successful in avoiding the assignment and this same behavior is more likely to happen next time he is given something to read.

The *Back in My Day* Theory

Whenever I give a training to a large group, there is invariably one person who brings up what I call the *Back in My Day* Theory. This theory is usually articulated like this: "Back in my day, the teacher had a paddle, and if we acted up, she took us out behind the school and whupped us with it until we behaved. Boy, if we could only do that today we would not have half the problems we do now! Kids these days wouldn't dare act up if they knew they were going to get the paddle."

The essential argument of the *Back in My Day* Theory is that our loss of paddling and other severe consequences is the reason we have so many behavior problems. It is a compelling theory, and many people from politicians to some teachers will tell you that if only we had a big paddle hanging on the wall, we would see far less of this misbehavior. Before you wind up subscribing to this idea, here are a few things to think about:

- Prior to the advent of IDEA, Section 504, and other disability laws, there were no protections for students with emotional and behavioral problems in our schools. Students who acted up were punished, and when that didn't work, those students were kicked out of school permanently. In effect, if the paddle didn't work, the student was sent off to reform school and you were left with only those students for whom it did work.

- Many students who have behavior problems already come from homes that are abusive, neglectful, or at least use corporal punishment. For these students, the threat of a paddle is not very intimidating.

- Students with emotional and behavioral disabilities do not have the ability to suddenly suppress their behavior to avoid a punishment. The impulsivity associated with most behavioral problems has lead to chronic failure and many social and academic consequences. If they could have avoided this by now, they probably would have.

- Punishment may suppress behavior, but it does not teach complex skills like organization, critical thinking, or impulse control. Punishment will not be successful in remediating deficits of any kind.

- Punishment destroys the relationship between the student and staff; it teaches students to avoid punishment and fear instructional staff rather than engage with them in healthy ways.

In addition to all these reasons, corporal punishment is banned in most states and is considered abuse. While it is tempting to think how the paddle may have once been a simple solution, in today's complex world of education it is a relic that we are better off without.

Addressing Behavior : The Key Components

The easiest way to manage behavior is to step back from the behavior itself and operate from effective principles. The hardest way to manage behavior is to react to the behavior and work from your emotional reaction.

We are going to start by discussing four core components of effective behavior interventions. What you may notice is that three of the four components don't occur *during* an episode of misbehavior but are preventive measures.

It is common for participants in workshops to ask me what to do during some nightmare scenario in which a student has escalated beyond control and is engaging in a severe behavior like throwing chairs. They want to know what to do when things are at their absolute worst and their options are already limited. You will know how to handle these situations by the time you finish this book, and you will have a host of new responses to a wide range of behaviors. However, you will also learn that behavior is much easier to prevent in its early stages by using proactive strategies.

There are four key components to managing and preventing disruptive behavior. We will examine each of these components in detail in the upcoming chapters, starting with structure and consistency.

Key Components of Behavior Support

- Structure and Consistency
- Positive and Proactive Strategies
- Relationship
- Appropriate Response

STRUCTURE AND CONSISTENCY

Structure

Providing *structure* means giving students a very clear idea of what is expected (e.g., rules and group agreements), what will happen and when (e.g., schedules and routines), and how things will happen (e.g., procedures). I like to say that structure answers "who, what, when, where, and how" questions.

- Who is allowed to use the computer?
- When is lunch?
- Where do we line up?
- What are the rules?
- How do I ask for a break?
- What happens if I break a rule?

Structure makes life orderly and predictable. Students with behavior issues often have a lot of problems transitioning from one activity to the next or coping with demands that are unexpected. Many students also lack the ability to solve problems and make appropriate decisions. As adults, we may be tempted to think of structure as boring or inhibiting. We may think it stifles students' creativity and free will. In general, however, the more serious and chronic a student's behavioral difficulties are, the more structure will benefit her.

Paraprofessionals often work individually with students. Even in these relationships, structuring your tasks and expectations can be very helpful for the student. Imagine, for instance, that you are assigned to work with a student on math. How often will you take a break? What type of effort do you expect? What happens if the student does not put forth the effort? Would you rather answer these questions before you start working with this student or renegotiate them every day?

> ### An example of structuring
>
> "Josh, I'm going to be tutoring you on this math lesson for the next three weeks. It's important for me that you don't get too bored or too frustrated because we are going too slow or too fast. How often do you think we should take a break? How many problems do you think you can do in one sitting? Do you want help, or should I back off after I show you how? If you seem distracted, what is the best way to help you get back on track?"

Notice in the box above that the paraprofessional is seeking to collaborate with the student by asking what works for him. She is providing him with some power to make choices and seeking agreement. She could have said, "You're going to do fifteen problems before you take a break," or "You can't take a break until you do fifteen problems." How much more successful do you think this staff member is going to be by engaging Josh in creating the structure rather than handing it to him?

Structure often means that even the most regular and mundane of activities are ordered by some procedure. The younger the student is, and the more intense his or her needs are, the more structure is important. High school students can handle walking from one class to another as a group; elementary school students travel in lines. In one class I visited recently there were even footprints on the floor to guide the kindergartners when lining up. This made the line straight and spaced evenly without the teacher having to verbally remind them of line etiquette every time. This simple procedure prevented a lot of wasted time and conflict.

Another aspect of structure means that there is rarely nothing at all to do. Idle time for students who don't know how to manage themselves is usually a bad idea. This means even free time has to be structured. You might say, for instance, "We have ten minutes of free time; you can be at your desk working quietly, at the back table playing a game, or on the computer if your work is done."

This is perfectly acceptable and, indeed, helpful. Some teachers may argue this doesn't teach self-management skills, and they are right. But setting students up by giving them too much leeway without expectations and correcting them when they fail, isn't really teaching them either. Learning self-management should progress one small step at a time. Children learn through a series of successes, not a series of failures and reminders.

Structure also means having a plan that details how you are going to respond to behavior. In addition to rules, you will need a general management strategy for what you will do in response to behaviors as they occur. In the second part of this book we will discuss effective reactions to behavior.

Consistency

Consistency means holding onto your expectations, but it does not mean being rigid or inflexible. Student misbehavior arises from a lack of skills to succeed, not lack of enforcement. Consistency is a *support* we provide to help students feel comfortable, understand rules and predict their environment. Inconsistent expectations and follow through is especially difficult for students to understand. Below are some common reasons staff members may be inconsistent with their expectations of students.

Common Causes of Inconsistency

- Wanting to be liked by students
- Feeling that enforcing the rules is "mean"
- Fearing a confrontation with the student
- Being too tired or busy to follow through
- Fearing being wrong about the issue
- Feeling uncertain if it is your role to address the behaivor

---

To demonstrate the effect of inconsistency, let's take the example of the family dog. Imagine that you decide you no longer wish to feed the family dog from the table. You stop giving away juicy morsels of steak. The dog still comes to the table and tries his puppy eyes on you. How long will it take for the dog to give up? A week? A month? The answer really depends on how *consistent* you are in holding onto your expectation that the dog does not eat from the table. What happens if not often, but occasionally, you give in? You might think your dog learns that every now and then you make a friendly and loving exception to the rule and that you are a kind and generous owner. What really happens is that your dog becomes confused. If he learns anything, he learns that to get his needs met he needs to beg more. Lacking the skill to speak or cook a steak himself he might think, "Every now and again, my owner gives me food from the table. Thus it takes about nine stern rebukes until I get to eat the occasional piece of steak." In the dog world, this is a deal! He also may sense that on some days, when you are tired and weary, you are more likely to dispense food. Even worse, let's say he yaps, barks, and howls until you just want to enjoy a peaceful dinner and you give in! He learns, "Sometimes to get my point across, I just need to yap and howl louder."

Let's apply the same logic to a student you work with. If you hold out your expectations and then fail to pursue them what do you think will happen? Say you have a rule that students may not bring music players to class. Then, one day, on a Friday, when you are tired, a student brings an iPod ® to your reading group and turns it on. You let it slide. From then on, every day, students will ask if it's OK to bring a music player they can listen to while they "work."

This is not to say that you might never allow a student to listen to music. The much wiser way to handle this would be to say, "Next Friday, those who have completed their work will be able to bring music players to class and listen to music with headphones. If it works out well, we may do it again." Notice that in this example, you have deliberately allowed music players (not ignored the rule) and created some structure (players must have headphones, work must be completed first). The important difference here is that you did not just "let it slide."

Consistency does not just apply to rule enforcement, it applies to everything. If you promise to have a conversation with a student later, offer him or her an incentive for completing work, or say that you will bring in a picture of your dog—*do it!* The trust and respect of students with behavior problems is hard to earn. Never miss an opportunity.

POSITIVE AND PROACTIVE ENVIRONMENT

Transforming challenging behavior requires the creation of an extraordinarily positive environment. A positive environment consists of two separate but related components: (1) a positive atmosphere and (2) positive, proactive discipline.

Positive Atmosphere

Creating a positive atmosphere is an essential component of changing behavior. Whether that atmosphere is in a classroom or a small group, on a bus, on a playground, or just between you and a student during a tutoring session, a positive environment encourages appropriate behavior.

A positive environment doesn't necessarily mean students will find every activity fun. You don't have to give out candy or prizes. It does mean that you as the adult are positive about the experience, refrain from negative comments, encourage students to do their best, and show an interest in students as people (not just in their performance).

Positive is not the absence of negative. You don't have a positive environment just because you aren't a downer of a person or because you don't openly berate students. Positive *is the presence of* truly *positive, happy, fulfilling, engaging, and welcoming energy*. It has to be so positive it drowns out the negative energy many students may try to bring in. This doesn't necessarily require a lot of charm or pep. Positivity can be presented at any pace and any volume.

A positive environment is one that is friendly to the students. It is never adversarial. It is never you trying to make the students behave. It is you trying to help and get to know them, giving them positive messages, believing in them, and showing it. This doesn't mean letting students do what they want. An environment can be positive and still hold students to a behavioral standard.

In the spring of 2006 I went to consult with a high school behavior program on the Oregon Coast. The students there had some of the best attendance I had ever seen. I was curious about how this program had such great success. The teacher was a young guy, and I asked him how he managed to keep his students coming.

"Every morning," he explained, "when the students come through the door, they get to mark a check next to their name on the board. When they have ten days in a row, I buy them a breakfast burrito." The teacher pointed to the names on the board. A few minutes later the students started coming in. Sure enough, every one arrived. Could this teacher have solved the nagging attendance problem of many behavior classrooms in America for the low cost $3.95 every two weeks? If he had, this would be an outstanding savings to many districts. The teacher greeted students enthusiastically as each one arrived.

"Glad to see you," he would say, "Welcome to class." Most kids asked if they could write their check mark up on the board. If a student didn't, the teacher

quickly encouraged him to mark himself present. He was very happy to see each student walk through that door, and he was very obvious about it.

Then I got it. This teacher had solved his attendance problem for free. The burrito was just a prop. The real magic was that every time those kids passed through that doorway, something positive happened. They were coming for the praise and the energy of the classroom that this young teacher had created.

How much different do you think this teacher's results would be if instead he said, "Well, look who finally decided to show up today," or "Where is your homework?" right as they walked through the door?

Positive, Proactive Discipline

When working with students is it better to encourage good behavior with incentives or punish bad behavior with consequences? What is positive discipline? Is it some weak-kneed approach that pampers students? Is it all sunshine and optimism that sounds good but is doomed to fail? Will the kids walk on you if you're just a "positive" person and don't make them pay the price for their behavior? These are all good questions that I hear a lot from teachers and paraprofessionals. We are going to spend a few minutes getting to the heart of these essential questions. First, let's go over a few terms.

Rewards

- Rewards are things we give students after they have done what they were supposed to do. For example, we might give a student who has turned in all the homework for the week a reward of extra recess on Friday.

Consequences

- Consquences are negatives imposed on the student for not performing a desired behavior (or performing an undesirable one). For example, a student who wastes time in class might be asked to leave the class and the time he is out might come off his recess later.

Reinforcers

- Reinforcers are different from rewards. The idea behind a reinforcer is to encourage the continuation of a desired behavior. This makes it different from a reward in two important ways. First, they occur during, not after, the behavior. Second, reinforcers may be used to show students they are coming closer to the desired behavior. For example, a staff member may see a student working on her homework, walk by and smile, and give that student a thumbs-up or a token even though that student has not completed the work yet.

Rewards: Using rewards as incentives assumes the student has the necessary skills to be successful but lacks proper motivation. Students are trying to meet basic important needs with behavior. Usually they are doing this in the quickest way they can. If they want attention they will take it *now*. If they want power or control, they will take it *now*. And if they want to avoid failure, they will avoid the assignment that is in front of them, *now*. The problem with long-term incentives and rewards (even things at the end of the day) is that many students with disruptive behaviors are not able to regulate their behavior by planning for things in the near future. They are much more interested in meeting their immediate emotional needs.

Consequences: Consequences suppress behavior. They don't teach a new behavior (unless you count new ways to escape and avoid consequences). They especially don't teach complicated skills like planning and social reasoning. For this reason, consequences are best used secondary to skill building and reinforcement. That is to say, use them to stop behaviors that are worth stopping: aggression, serious disruptions and bullying, things that undermine the classroom's safety and positive environment. The impact of consequences is generally temporary and disappears as soon as the person imposing them leaves the room. On the other hand, some form of consequences are necessary to maintain a sense of order and fairness in the classroom. To this degree, consequences have their place. The important thing to remember about consequences is not to expect them to be agents of change.

There is a temptation to think that huge consequences will have a bigger impact on students. The truth is they do not. The problem is that students who are short-term oriented do not perceive the impact of consequences in the future very well. There are two reasons big ugly consequences don't work very well. First, consequences based on *fear* (e.g. threatening the student with a referral to the office) lose their value once the consequence has been applied. Second, consequences based on duration (e.g. losing recess for a month) lose their value quickly once the student gets used to it.

Reinforcers: Positive reinforcement is one way to teach behaviors. Behaviors that are reinforced are more likely to be repeated in the future. Reinforcement can take a variety of different forms. The most common, easiest, cheapest and most effective, is praise. You can use reinforcement to let students know when they are displaying successful behaviors. Sometimes people think that people should not be praising students for behaviors they should already be doing. Nothing is further from the truth. We want to be focusing on and encouraging the behaviors we like.

Recently a student who was very upset confronted me. "I hate you Dr. Henson! I'm $%$%ed off at you for giving me this stupid $%$#&$ work!" My response to him was this: "Hey, it sounds like you are pretty frustrated with this assignment and with me. I appreciate that you can tell me why you're mad. It's not exactly how I want to hear it but let's figure this out." I managed to praise the behavior I wanted to see more of (expressing the reason he was angry) without reacting to the invitation to power struggle or kicking him out of the class, where I'm sure no work would have been accomplished. Did he still have to do the work? You bet! And he got, per the teacher's rules, a negative to his participation grade for swearing.

It's also common for students in more intensive behavior programs to have a reinforcement system in which they earn tokens or points for doing the right thing and later cash these in for rewards. You may also see school-wide reinforcement systems where desired behaviors are recognized and rewarded with tickets that are exchanged for prizes. The core of any reinforcement is not the prizes. It is the human interaction, the adult giving the students direct, positive feedback.

The ability to praise effectively, not just praise, is essential for teaching new behaviors. It is important that you praise a student for behaviors you want to see more of. Never praise substandard work or behavior. Praise must always be sincere to be of any value. Students from kindergarten on can tell the difference between sincere and insincere praise. Try to praise very specifically so that students get good feedback on exactly what they are doing right. Finally, make sure that your praise is at least a 8:1 ratio to any negative feedback you must give students.

Examine the examples below. Which praising statements to you think are more effective at teaching a student new skills?

- Good job!

- Hey, I know you didn't want to do this, but you got 6 problems done already! I like your motivation.

- Good choice!
- I like the way your binder is neatly organized.
- You made a great decision just then ignoring that comment and heading back to your desk.
- The way you said that, in a calm tone, really made me want to listen to what you were saying.

Proactive Engagement

Another important component of managing behavior is to be proactive in the way you handle behavior. This means you are endeavoring to prevent misbehavior and encourage appropriate behavior. Proactive engagement also means that you are taking time to construct the physical and emotional environment of your class in a way that makes students feel safe and welcome.

I once observed a classroom in which the teacher ran from one problem to the next. I watched as she put one student in time-out for shouting at her, and then ran over to another one who was crying because someone had taken apart his Lego ® toy. Then she confronted two students who were talking. When the class finally settled down she flopped down in her chair, exhausted. "Now I can finally relax," she said.

This is the way behavior is often handled. Unfortunately, it is a terribly hard way to do it. Being proactive means being *active* with your students and this means all the time, especially when all is going well. Below is a list of proactive management techniques that you can be using *all the time!*

Proactive Management Strategies

- Praise: Let students who are doing well know it! This also helps others remember the expectations. You can also praise the class by making a comment to your co-workers about how well a student or group of students is doing.

- Proximity: Walk up and down the aisles of the class, positioning yourself close to potential trouble spots.

- Environment: Seat students in areas you know will produce the least amount of distraction and conflict.

- Prepare: Make sure students understand how much time they have left and how soon they will be transitioning to the next activity. Many students with behavior problems have an especially difficult time with transitions.

- Smile: Believe it or not, your mood affects the mood and demeanor of the room.

Positive Language

Another way to create a positive environment is through the language we use. We can say the same things in many different ways. If we want students to hear us, positive language works better. Imagine all the ways you can ask a student to take a seat.

- "Get back in your chair!"

- "Why are you up out of your seat when you know it's time for spelling?"

- "Could you please not be up and running around?"
- "Could you please take a seat?"

If you were a student, which one would you prefer? Personally, I like the last one. Now think of all the different ways you could say this. You could say it with a sharp tone, nicely, meekly, or with some annoyance in our voice. You could say it in a whine, or apologetically, or you could say it calmly and with confidence. Which do you think would work the best?

Another common way to phrase a confrontation is called the "I" statement. The "I" statement is designed to provoke less defensiveness. The simple formula is: "I _____ when _____."
For example, "I find it difficult to teach when my students are out of their seats." This phrasing avoids any blame of the other person and talks about what the speaker is experiencing. Many people find this way of talking useful in working with students who react strongly to any confrontation. Many of us are used to "you statements" such as, "You are out of your seat," "You need to stop," or "You are going to get in big trouble!" The one word an "I" statement never contains is "you."

A form of communication I advise against is sarcasm. Many teachers and educational staff I have met have wonderful abilities to use sarcastic humor. This has its place in the staff lounge, but there are some good reasons not to use it with your students. First, if you don't want them to use it on you, don't use it on them. Young students don't get it. Students with communication disorders don't get it. Students with disorders that affect social information processing (such as Asperger's disorder) don't get it. Students whose parents don't use it don't get it. English language learners don't get it. Overall, it's not an effective way to communicate. If you're good at it, save it for after school.

The best language to use is positive language. This is language that talks about what the student can do, what is possible and what is expected. It is not about what is forbidden.

Negative Language	Positive Language
• You can't have recess until 11:00 a.m.	• We have recess at 11:00 a.m.
• Please don't leave a mess at your desk.	• Please clean up around your desks.
• I'm not going to listen to any disrespect from you!	• I will be happy to listen to you when you are speaking respectfully.

RELATIONSHIPS

The heart of working with any student is your relationship with him or her. You may have hours each day to build a relationship with a student or you may have only minutes. The success of everything you do, from teaching academics to addressing behavior, depends on the way that student perceives you. Students thrive on positive healthy relationships and fail without them. Often when people want to learn behavior management, they want to learn tips and techniques, nifty sayings, good consequences, and other tricks of the trade. The reality is that there are no techniques that substitute for a good relationship. Managing and changing disruptive behavior is, at its core, a relational experience.

Having a "good" relationship with a student does not mean you are his or her favorite staff member, or necessarily that it is a friendly or deep relationship. It does mean that the student respects you. Earning the respect of each student is done by acting consistently, fairly, and respectfully. One way to think of this relationship is as a bank account. Each time you act in a way the student can respect, you make a small deposit. Over time you build up an account. Now and again you may need to ask the student to behave differently. If you have built up a good account, the student is more likely to do so. If you have been unfair, inconsistent, or weak in the past you may have little balance to draw on.

One of the best ways to build a relationship with a student is to engage him or her in conversation about things that have nothing to do with academics or behavior. Spending a few minutes every week talking with students about what is important to them—from video games to music to their favorite pet—will do wonders to build a trusting relationship.

Over the years I've known many students who have come up through behavior programs and graduated. When I ask them what it was that made them successful they say two things. First, they had to make the choice on their own. Second, there was someone they trusted there to help them. Last year I was at a conference where a vice principal told me the following story:

Courtney

I had a student last year named Courtney who was always in trouble. She often skipped class, and there was hardly a week that went by when she didn't get herself in trouble mouthing off to a teacher. She and I had several knock-down, drag-out screaming matches last year. I suspended her three times. I must have talked to her ten or twenty times, and she always said she would try harder, but next week she was doing the same thing. I decided at the end of the year to let the other vice principal handle Courtney's discipline because she was causing me so much stress. When the students came back the next year I referred anything that had to do with Courtney to the other VP. Last week Courtney came into my office and said she wanted to talk to me.

"I'm really mad at you!" she said. "Last year you suspended me three times and I know we didn't get along, but at least you were there. This year you ignored me! That hurt worse than anything. That was the worst thing you could have done!"

Imagine the vice principal's surprise when Courtney told him how she was feeling. Courtney was the last person in the world he thought he had a meaningful relationship with. To me, this story illustrates an important point: we build relationships with students in everything we do, even while we are handling their misbehavior. It is critically important that we are fair and consistent and that we show we care.

Personal-Professional Boundaries

Most of us work in education because we like working with kids and enjoy the relationships we develop with students. There are, however, some important boundary lines that are very important to maintain with any student, especially when working with students with disruptive behaviors. The general rule is that *the more behavioral support a student needs, the more distinct your personal-professional boundaries must be*. There are several types of boundaries that are important to maintain.

Staff/Student Boundary: Positive relationships are essential in working with students who exhibit disruptive behaviors. However, a relationship with a student is not a friendship. It is important you maintain clarity with your students that you are a staff member. If students see you as a "buddy" or peer, they are

WHAT WOULD YOU SAY IF A STUDENT ASKED YOU?

You are my friend, right? You will get this question sooner or later and the answer you give is important. A good answer is something like this: "Well, actually, I am your teaching assistant, which is a little different than a friend. I like you, and I think there are a lot of neat things about you. My job, however, is to teach you, and sometimes that will mean doing things that friends don't do, like give out homework. Some days, you might not even like me!"

Have you ever had a beer? This, and variations on this question (have you ever...) is essentially a trap question whether the person asking intends it or not. It is a yes or no question to which there is no right answer. If you say no, you are a teetotaling Goody Two-Shoes who could not possibly know anything about the person's circumstances. If you say yes, you are an affirmed (and probably raging) alcoholic who has no business teaching. Don't try to lie your way out of this one either with the old "I had one once and didn't like it." Best answer: "I'm not sure what that question has to do with your math assignment."

Can I borrow a dollar? The answer to this question is always no. If the student professes to be starving, needs bus fare, or owes the local thugs a dollar, it is still no. If a student needs lunch or bus fare, you can help them by calling home. Sometimes staff will lend some money with collateral. Think about it this way: are you willing to lend and track collateral for ten students? Do you have any right to hold a student's iPod because you lent him two bucks? Think about it, and you will arrive at your own friendly version of no.

not likely to afford you much respect when you ask them to do (or stop doing) something.

This also means our relationships with students are not mutual. We don't expect them to do anything for us. We do not ask them for emotional support. We don't expect them to listen to our personal problems, empathize with our financial circumstances, or discuss our medical conditions. We don't offer students information about our conflicts with other staff members, our inside knowledge of school politics, or anything else that is not in their best interest to hear.

You *can* build warm, friendly, supportive, and helpful relationships with students by being a caring adult who takes an interest in them. Students need healthy relationships with appropriate boundaries to learn how to be successful young people.

Work/Home Boundary: An important part of the personal-professional boundary line is maintaining a distinction between your work and home life. Many districts have policies against contact with students outside of school, including driving students to and from school. Many of these policies were created to protect students from inappropriate relationships and protect staff members from liability. It is not possible for you to spend time with *every* student outside of school. Therefore, spending time with any student can create the perception of favoritism. This can also be very confusing to students. Any contact with students outside of school should be approved on a case-by-case basis by the school administration, and take place with at least three people present. This protects you from liability and accusations of inappropriate relationships.

Self-Disclosure: The term "self-disclosure" means telling things that are of a personal nature to someone else. Self-disclosure with students can be very powerful and help them identify with you, or it can backfire in ways that destroy your reputation and credibility. There are two very important rules to follow for self-disclosure:

1. *Self-disclosure must always be in the student's best interest*.

2. *What you disclose should be something you don't mind being on the front page of tomorrow's paper.*

And I do mean the *front page*, not buried in the classified section. Students don't need to know certain information about you, but they will ask. It is perfectly OK to tell a student that the information they are asking is too personal or not appropriate for school.

It's not uncommon for educators to meet a student whose situation reminds them of their own struggles in school. Let's say you meet a student who has family problems and suffers from depression. You share that you also had a difficult childhood and suffer from depression. Will this help the student? Would you be OK if the student told the entire class you had "family problems" and were "depressed?" Would the student suddenly be able to relate to you or might they think, *How are you supposed to help me if you are depressed also?*

Self-disclosure is like the difference between a handsaw and a power saw. You can really get some work done quickly with a power saw. You can also cut your hand off. It is something you should not take a risk with. If you are uncertain that self-disclosure will help a student, hold off or discuss it with another staff member first.

Keeping Secrets: How would you reply if a student said, "I want to tell you a secret, but you have to promise not to tell anyone!"? You, of course, want to hear the secret, but what if the secret is something serious? There is going to be a fight after school behind the gym; the student is pregnant and hasn't told her parents; the student is being abused by an uncle; another student brought a knife to school; the student is planning to try drugs for the first time at a party this weekend. Depending on the information, your district's policies, and state law, a student may tell you something you are mandated to report. So what do you say? I recommend some variation of this: "I don't promise to keep secrets. There are some things that are serious that I may need to do something about. If you tell me, there is no guarantee I can keep it secret."

There are also things you may want other staff to know about. One handsome young paraprofessional I knew often received "crush" notes from girls in the middle school where he worked. He always made sure to tell another staff when he received one, and he kept copies of the notes in a file at school. If he were ever accused of any wrongdoing he could show that he does not maintain any "secret" relationships with students.

It does happen that students get crushes on staff members. This smart paraprofessional would say to his student, "I'm flattered. You understand, of course, me being an adult, and you being a student that this could never happen?" I feel it wise of him to include the word never so as to give a very clear message. It has been very effective at nipping many a crush where it began. It is unwise to let a student flatter you in any way about your looks or appeal. Always consider any attempt to do so inappropriate on the student's part and stop it.

To sum up this section on secret keeping, there are always some things you would never keep secret, and would immediately refer to a teacher, administrator, or mental health professional in order to get the student help. Below are some examples.

> ## Things You Would Never Keep Secret
> - Discussion, even casually, about suicide
> - Threats to hurt someone else
> - Observed incidents or reports of bullying
> - Disclosure or observed evidence of physical or sexual abuse
> - Disclosure or observed evidence of child neglect or endangerment
> - Any concern for the student's safety including plans to engage in unsafe behavior
> - Concern about the student's emotional well being
> - Concerns about an untreated medical condition
> - Writings or drawings that raise concern
> - Sexualized behavior by the student

Confidentiality: All of the information you learn about a student in the course of your job is protected by law. The heart of confidentiality is that what happens in your job stays there. You are in a position to know things about people that are very private: how good they are at academics, what kind of learning disability they have, where they live, what kind of medications they take, if they get free or reduced lunch. You may witness incidents with students that are funny to you but embarrassing to them.

There have been incidents in which school staff have gone to lunch and talked negatively about a student or a family, only to find out that a good friend of the family was eating lunch in the next booth! These kinds of incidents do worse than just embarrass you; they ruin the all the work you have done to help that student over the entire year and destroy your relationships with the student's parents.

Professionally, you never discuss students outside of work in a way that uses *any* information that could be used to identify that student. In public places, like restaurants, it is best to find other topics, even if you are with coworkers.

Giving Advice: Keep in mind the professional limitations of your role with the student; this is another important boundary. In my private practice as a consulting psychologist, I am asked a lot of questions about things I know just a little about. I get asked regularly to provide legal advice to parents, make decisions about the appropriateness of a student's medication, or decide on the best educational curriculum for a classroom. These are all things that are outside my professional scope as a psychologist. Even when I do have an opinion, I refer the question to a lawyer, psychiatrist, or teacher. Why? Because, despite my *personal* experience and opinion, I don't have the credentials to make those decisions.

When working with students, you may sometimes be placed in the role of a therapist. Students may come to you with any number of issues. They may even be issues you know something about. In cases like these, it is not your role to give advice to the student. The most important thing you might do is listen and empathize. It is also beyond the scope of your job to give medical, legal, nutritional, dietary, or any other type of advice. Doing so could land you in legal hot water as well as harm the student *even if the advice is correct.* When a student's problems are beyond your role, refer the matter to the student's teacher or counselor and allow him or her to make a referral to the appropriate expert.

Below is a table that I hope will help you sort out the important difference between helping a student process feelings and what might be considered therapy.

Process (within your role)	Therapy (outside your role)
• Listening • Empathizing • Repeating, reframing • Asking questions • Addressing immediate issues (what the student will do next)	• Discussing or giving advice on any number of issues including treatment of mental conditions, family problems, or addictions • Telling a student you think he or she has a medical or psychological condition or disability

You may encounter some students who enjoy almost endless processing of their feelings. These students have a new "problem" every day and need to talk about it extensively. At first, this can feel good, as the student is very grateful for someone to talk to. However, if you find this happening every day, chances are that the student is avoiding academics and using you largely as a way out of something else. Don't be sucked in to playing therapist. Set boundaries around when and how long students can process with you.

Examples of Boundary Violations

- *Staff/Student*
  - Seeking emotional support from a student
  - Telling a student you don't like the principal
- *Work/Home*
  - Calling a student at home "just to chat"
  - Driving a student home
- *Self-Disclosure*
  - Telling a student about your divorce
  - Telling a student you used drugs in college
- *Keeping Secrets*
  - Agreeing to keep any secret when you don't know what it is
  - Agreeing not to tell the teacher the student skipped class
- *Confidentiality*
  - Telling one parent information about the parents of another student
  - Telling your neighbor stories about the students you work with
- *Giving Advice*
  - Advising a student with diabetes on how to lose weight
  - Playing therapist to a student who is depressed

APPROPRIATE RESPONSE
TO BEHAVIOR

We have spent the first part of this book learning about behavior, the reasons it may occur, and how to prevent misbehavior by maintaining a structured, positive, and proactive focus and developing healthy, empathic relationships. Still, these interventions won't prevent all misbehavior. How you react to unwanted behaviors is a critical component in determining whether you will see those behaviors again and how often you will see them.

A Win-Win Model

Many students with misbehavior are accustomed to a *win-lose* mentality of interacting with adults. Every disagreement is a battle where one person wins, and the other loses. No one likes to lose; kids don't and you don't. If every interaction results in a staff or a student feeling resentful because they were trumped, there will rarely be any peace! It is vital that you interact with students in ways that create *win-win* situations. Imagine these two ways of addressing a student who refuses to work.

- *"Jason, you have to get this work done. I'm not going to let you use the computer until it's done. I'm serious about this. You are not going to sit here and get away with doing nothing and then go play. No work, no computer!"*

- *"Jason, I know this work is hard for you. I want to help you get it done so you can use the computer. How do you think we could finish this so you can have some time to do what's important to you?"*

In the first example, the staff member has taken a firm stand. If Jason does the work, Jason loses the battle with the staff member. In the later example, no one loses any face whether the work is done or not done. If you are coercive with students, you can expect them to react by opposing you. If you act collaboratively toward students, they are less likely to engage in battle.

Ways to Provoke a Battle with Students
- Threaten to give them a consequence
- Raise your voice
- Look annoyed and frustrated
- Try to bribe them
- Act disappointed in the student
- Act as if you are desperate and disempowered
- Posture yourself in a threatening way
- Confront them in front of an audience

Management Styles

There are some styles that work with managing behavior and some that do not. The best way to handle misbehavior is to have a preplanned system for addressing behavior. Students should know what type of response to expect from staff members when their behavior is inappropriate.

There are some very ineffective and inefficient ways to address behavior. Usually ineffective systems develop when there is no system in place to start with. Three of the most common ineffective systems are management by crisis, management by personality, and management by loyalty.

The **crisis** style of management involves running from one crisis or misbehavior to the next, making your focus what is going wrong rather than what is going right. It's a high-speed, exhausting style that may seem necessary but in the end creates more work and more misbehavior.

The **personality** style of management involves using wit, charm, humor, and quick fixes in lieu of maintaining structure, consistency, and agreements. Everything is flexible, negotiable, and subject to the interpretation of the staff member. Most things are done "on the fly." While having a good personality is definitely an advantage in working with students, using it to the exclusion of set expectations will cause you problems.

The **loyalty** model involves creating an atmosphere based only on relationships between people, not on any rules, agreements, or structure. Students are given the message that misbehavior will compromise the relationship between themselves and the staff member. The loyalty model is especially easy to fall into when you often work one-on-one with the same student.

In contrast, management by system has clear advantages. Let's compare these side by side and see how creating a system can be advantageous in many ways.

Management by Crisis	Management by System
• Relies on intervention (not prevention) to manage behavior • Addresses misbehavior on the student's terms, not the staff member's terms • Automatically gives students attention for misbehavior	• Relies on prevention and proactive measures to manage behavior • Manages behavior before it escalates into a problem • Manages misbehavior in ways that make it less likely to occur again

Management by Personality	Management by System
• Relies on personality, charm, humor, and quick fixes to problems • Varies with the mood and energy level of the staff member • Varies greatly among staff members • Can't be replicated by anyone else when that staff member is not present	• Relies on predetermined rules, agreements, and methods to manage behavior • Maintains consistency among staff members • Is usable by anyone with minimal training

Management by Loyalty	Management by System
• Based on reciprocal interaction and guilt	• Student's relationship with staff members is based on their role as educators
• Relies completely on the relationship with the student, not the expectations or rules	• The relationship with the student does not supersede what is expected of him or her
• Doesn't work well with all students	• Maintains the flexibility to be effective with all students
• Students can punish staff with misbehavior	• Maintains consistency among staff members
• Less professional	
• Varies with personalities of staff members	

Choosing a Response to Behavior

When a misbehavior occurs, despite all your proactive strategies, how you respond to it is very important. The first decision you will want to make is what kind of behavior you are experiencing. There are three basic types:

Crisis: A crisis is a threat to health and safety. If two students get into a fight or a student runs into a busy street, you have a crisis. Students in crisis require certain interventions and the use of crisis management skills. During a crisis the focus of the staff member is to *negate the threat*. Staff members are not concerned with implementing discipline or trying to make the event into a teachable moment; these actions could potentially escalate the situation.

Unwanted Behavior: An unwanted behavior can express itself in a number of ways. The behavior may be intentional (a student throws a piece of paper at another student's head) or unintentional (a student with ADHD is out of his seat, wandering around). The behavior may be severe (a student cursing and screaming at the teacher) or mild (chewing gum). The reaction of staff during a behavior episode should generally involve using their behavior response system. They should be careful not to overreact or over attend to a behavior. They do not necessarily need to engage in teaching, although they might, depending on the circumstance and the student.

Teachable Moment: A teachable moment is a time in which a student's misbehavior is the result of honestly not knowing the proper way to handle a situation and in which the student is potentially receptive to learning. Imagine that a student hurls a wad of crumpled paper at the back of another student's head. Does he really need a lecture on rules or the reasons not to throw paper? Probably not. In contrast, a student who is loudly demanding to use the computer might respond to "Let's start by lowering your voice and put that in a question…Great! I like that much better."

Knowing what type of situation you are dealing with will help you determine your response. The boxes below may give you some ideas on how to react in different situations.

Crisis	Unwanted Behavior	Teachable Moment
• Intervene • De-escalate • Prevent injury • Manage escalation	• Provide structure • Maintain consistency with expectations • Attempt win-win solutions • Praise/ reinforce appropriate behaviors • Respond accordingly to the percieved funtion of the behavior • Use established discipline system	• Process • Discuss • Teach • Review expectations • Demonstrate • Role Model

Creating a Response System

You should have a simple, pre-established method for handling behavior. You may work in some locations where a system has already been established. Where a behavior system already exists, it is important you get to know how it works by discussing it with the staff members who use it. Where nothing exists, it may be beneficial for you to help create a very simple behavior response system. To do this you will need to answer some key questions:

1. What are the expectations, rules, and agreements students are expected to follow?

61

2. What will staff members do in response to violations?

3. How will you handle continued misbehavior, escalation, or defiance?

Staff members need a continuum of responses, as students may continue behaviors or escalate in response to being confronted. What will you do if a student runs down the hall? What will you do if she refuses to stop when you ask her? What will you do if she runs from you? If you catch up to her, then what? What if she does it again the next day?

Generally you want your continuum of interventions to start with the least restrictive intervention possible. If a student can be steered away from misbehavior by a gentle reminder, why bother with a stern warning? Below is a sample response system and following that is a continuum of techniques that may be useful in developing responses to misbehavior.

Response System: A Sample Story

A playground assistant often had problems with students from the third grade playing too roughly at recess. She tried reminding them each time, but the boys insisted on wrestling, slap-boxing, or playing tackle football. Each time she asked them to stop, the boys would behave for a short while and then, almost deliberately, do it again. She got permission from the vice principal to implement a new system. That night she went out and purchased a whistle. The next day students were informed of the new policy. One whistle was a warning to stop whatever they were doing.

A second whistle, which was two blows, meant they had to spend five minutes sitting up against the wall with the playground assistant. If they got another whistle that recess, their recess was over!

On the first day the boys again began playing roughly. The assistant blew the whistle and the boys barely seemed to listen, so she went down and interrupted their game.

"That's one warning," she told them. The boys did not seem concerned. One of them even snickered. "I don't feel like you are talking this seriously," she said to the snickering boy and blew the whistle twice more. "That's the second whistle for you." The boy went up to sit against the wall. The other boys resumed playing and the assistant was barely back to her chair before another boy was acting unsafely. She took a second boy out, careful to seat him far enough away from the other one that they would not talk. Now she had a chance to work on the first one with some collaborative energy.

"I want to make sure you have a good time," she said. The boy acted as if he didn't hear. "It looks like you guys are having a lot of fun, but I also need you to be safe. Can you make sure that you and all your friends don't get another whistle?" The boy still acted nonchalantly. After five minutes she sent him back.

The game resumed and this time it went for a while, until once again they were tackling each other. At this point she took the offending boy out again, and he lost recess for the rest of the day. The other boys quieted down a bit after this.

In the next several weeks, the assistant had to take the boys out several more times. After they learned what would happen, and the plan was implemented consistently, their rough behavior decreased until thirty days later she was almost never blowing the whistle on them.

You can see from the story above how the assistant developed some quick behavioral strategies, obtained approval for them, pretaught them to the students, and then used them effectively. She also didn't put up with any disrespect. When she sensed a student wasn't taking her seriously, she gave him a time-out.

What could she do if the boys refused to stop? What if they ignored the playground assistant altogether and just kept on playing roughly? The assistant would have a plan in case the boys were especially disrespectful or defiant. She might, for example, refer them to the vice principal, who might call their parents, restrict their recess privileges, or impose another consequence.

The playground assistant would also be using methods other than just a whistle. These might include (a) being consistent in the way she blows the whistle with these and other students; (b) building relationships with these students when she has the opportunity, for instance, when they are sitting against the wall; (c) taking a win-win attitude: "I want you to have a good time, but also be safe," not a "behave or lose your recess" attitude; and (d) praising the students when they do well.

A Continuum of Selected Behavioral Techniques

There are many different techniques you can use in response to an unwanted behavior. These interventions form a "tool kit" of responses you can draw from. They are listed starting with the least intrusive techniques and progress into more directive measures. Each technique also has an example of how it could be used effectively in a situation. In the following pages we will discuss many tools you can add to your tool kit. These will give you a wider range of responses to behaviors you may encounter.

Selective Ignoring: Sometimes it is easier to ignore a behavior than engage with it. Use this technique when the behavior is likely to end (and not repeat) and is relatively minor.

- A student who is asked to read a chapter yells, "No, I won't!" but then gets the book out, sits down with a sigh and opens the book. Do you really need to address the defiant comment when he is doing what you asked anyway?
- Students are not supposed to get out of their seats. A student stands up and stretches then sits back down to work. Is it worth it to confront her about such a brief time out of her chair?

Proximity: A proximity intervention is one in which you maintain a position close to a student or group of students prone to acting out behaviors. Often, posting yourself in the right spot, or moving around among students, will prevent you from having to intervene.

- A paraprofessional seats himself right next to a student who often gets into conflicts at the lunch table.
- A librarian sees two students starting to argue over a book. She stands near them and they tone their language down.

Cross Talk: Cross talk is talk between staff members that is intended for students to "overhear." For cross talk to be effective, it's common for both staff members to understand that it is taking place. Cross talk is not directed at the student but intended to inform, praise, or encourage him. It is not a backward or passive way to apply discipline. Use this technique to convey information or remind.

- Students in a math group know that they need to complete the day's assignment. If they do, it is possible they will have some free time at the end of the period. Several groups of students are talking. One staff member says to the other, "I really hope this group can pull it together and earn some free time."
- Two instructional assistants, one new and one experienced, are waiting for a line of kindergarten students to quiet down before they move them through the halls to the

cafeteria. Two boys are still talking. Rather than reprimand the boys, the experienced staff member says to the other, "Right now what we are doing is waiting for the line to be quiet. When it's all quiet, we will go."

Praise: Praising appropriate behavior, in general, is a better tactic than criticizing negative behavior. Sometimes you can get students to correct a behavior by praising and complimenting others who are already doing it. Use this technique to really praise students who are doing well, not to make backward comments such as, "I see at least *some* people are working."

- A teacher writes an assignment on the board and instructs students to copy it. When she notices that a few students are fidgeting or passing notes instead of copying, she says, "I see a lot of you are doing a really great job copying the day's assignment off the white board."
- An assistant trying to get a line of kindergartners quiet says, "I see William, Milly, and Katherine are standing quietly, great job. Oh, I also see Edward standing quietly! Who else can I find that is standing quietly?"

Shaping: The idea behind a technique called shaping is to praise the behavior you like even when, overall, a student's behavior does not meet the expectation. It is a variation of praising appropriate behavior that is directed at the student, not others around him or her. Shaping can seem like praising substandard behavior; however, the key element of shaping a behavior is to reinforce the small behaviors a student is doing that are appropriate. Use this technique to teach appropriate behaviors.

- A student is known for her angry temper. She often yells and screams whenever she is corrected on any academic work. The teacher hands a worksheet back to her to correct. Seeing the red marks, the student lets out a big sigh and stomps off. The paraprofessional says, "You handled that much better this time than before." He knows the student still needs to improve but decides he will get more mileage out of praising the improvement rather than being critical of the attitude.

- A student who does little work walks through the door that morning with his notebook. The paraprofessional spots him and says, "Hey, Michael! I'm really glad you came to class today. I see you brought your notebook. Fantastic!"

Non-Verbal Prompt: It is often the case that a nonverbal interaction creates less resistance from a student than a verbal one. Students who are prone to arguing and contradicting staff members have a much harder time responding this way to a nonverbal instruction. If you are going to use a gesture, it is important to preteach the meaning so students understand what is expected when they see it.

- A student is getting noisy in the cafeteria. The monitor walks by the table and uses her hand to make a gesture to the student. The students have been pretaught that this is a cue to quiet down.
- A class of students is working quietly when one student begins to hum. The staff member walks by and quietly touches him on the shoulder. He recognizes this as a cue to stop. (Remember, however, that not all students appreciate and some react strongly to any touch).

Verbal Prompting: There comes a point when behavior needs to be addressed directly. This is probably the most commonly used form of behavioral interaction. It involves simply asking the student to stop the behavior or engage in a different behavior.

- "Would you please return to your seat?"
- "Would you please work on this quietly?"

Warning/Direction: Students engaging in certain behaviors may need a warning or stern direction. A warning often implies that a consequence will follow. This is not a threat; it is what they are to understand as their "last" reminder. Warnings are used only once; they are used to draw a line when and where a line needs to be drawn. Warnings work only if you can and will back them up. The problem with warnings and directions is that they can increase resistance from the student. Use them sparingly. Sometimes a stern direction works better.

Will Henson, Psy.D.

- A student has continued to talk after being asked not to. The staff member says, "I've asked you to stop. If I need to ask you again, I am going to ask you to move over here by me."
- Two students are arguing and it seems they are posturing for a fight. The staff member asks them to separate but they continue to escalate with their words. The staff member moves closer and says, "You go sit there, and you go to that corner of the room."

Time-Out: The time-out procedure is one in which the student takes a few minutes away from other students and activities. Time-outs are most frequently used as part of classrooms where behavior is an issue. This is a brief time, usually two to five minutes, during which the student is expected to demonstrate certain behaviors and not engage in any activities. Time-out, like most interventions, should be pretaught to students so they understand what is expected. It is very hard to teach a student how to take a time-out at the moment they need one! Use time-outs when less restrictive measures have failed and the student is continuing to cause problems. There are several important points to understand about time-outs, listed below.

A. Have a time-out area that is free from distractions, such as magazines and toys, and away from loose objects, which students might destroy or throw. The time-out area should be a place where staff can observe the student but the student does

70

not have direct eye contact with the rest of the class. Some common time-out spots include a cubical or partitioned area, a space right outside the classroom door, or a space up against a building wall if outside. Avoid any possible humiliation, such as forcing a student to stand in a corner.

B. The staff should set clear parameters on what constitutes a time-out. A time-out should be used when behavior is disruptive. There is no need to give a student a time-out for sitting quietly (even if she is not working) or failing to turn in an assignment.

C. All staff should give time-outs to students in the same ways. They should use the same language, the same time-out spots, and the same methods of letting students know they are on track for a time-out. If your work setting uses time-outs as part of a classroom management strategy, it is important to familiarize yourself with the procedure.

D. A time-out starts when the student is quiet and respectfully requests that the staff member start his time. Two minutes sitting in a chair screaming obscenities is not a time-out. The student is expected to be quiet and not talk or communicate in any way (including eye rolling, heavy sighs, banging, or kicking). If he talks or communicates in some way, his time starts over.

E. Staff members do not communicate with the student during a time-out. They don't process why the student is upset. They simply say, "Let me know when you would like me to start your time," "I am starting your time," "I am starting your time over," etc. While this may seem somewhat harsh, understand that we generally give time-outs for defiant and oppositional behavior. By the time you have to give one, you won't have a student who is ready to talk. That student needs to take some time to reorient, and the staff needs not to engage.

F. After the time-out, staff may discuss the incident and help the student create a plan so the behavior won't recur.

Below is an example of the appropriate use of a time-out procedure.

• A student is being disruptive, wandering around the class and calling people "punks." The paraprofessional asks nicely, "Carlos, would you please return to your seat?" Carlos laughs and continues the behavior. The behavior is starting to seriously disrupt class. "Carlos, I am giving you a reminder now," the paraprofessional says. Carlos thinks about it and goes back to his seat but then puts his head down and mumbles "punk" under his breath. The paraprofessional says, "Carlos, please take a time-out now." Carlos is directed to the time-out area, a cubicle just outside the door. The paraprofessional goes out with him. All the while he is complaining that staff members are unfair and racist. The paraprofessional doesn't engage in this dialogue. He kicks the cubicle's underside and pouts for a few minutes.

The paraprofessional reminds him once, "When you are meeting the time-out expectations we can start your time." She doesn't hover and remind him over and over again. Carlos finally sits down. "Start my #$%&*$% time," he says. The paraprofessional doesn't respond. She knows Carlos knows that kind of request won't work. After a few minutes Carlos is calmer. "Fine, I'm ready," he says. The paraprofessional replies, "I'm starting your time." Carlos then mumbles "punk" under his breath to the staff. The staff replies, "I will start your time over." It takes awhile for Carlos to complete his time-out. After this the paraprofessional might process the incident with him briefly if she feels it would be helpful.

Consequences: Consequences should be used for deliberate behaviors (or at least avoidable ones). Consequences should not be used to punish a student for a behavior he or she cannot help. You can't, for example, punish a student who has ADHD (Attention Deficit Hyper-activity Disorder) for fidgeting in her seat. Mild consequences work well for most behaviors. We discussed earlier the importance of a *win-win* model of interaction with students. Thus, it is important that a staff member not convey the impression he is winning a battle against the student by giving the consequence. It is often the case that we as staff members want consequences so we don't feel defeated by students. This is the wrong reason to give a consequence.

So let's talk about how to give a consequence. First, it is *critical* that you have set the stage beforehand by letting students know what you expect, what the rules are, and how to be successful. Then it is no longer a battle between you and the student but between the student and her own impulses and behaviors. When she gets a consequence she then has no one but herself to blame.

It is also important to make sure students do not dig themselves a hole. I once knew a staff member in a group home who decided to give students a day of lunch detention for every swear word they said. He had to change his tune when one student racked up 133 days of lunch detention in two days.

- During a language arts exercise a student makes the comment, "This is #%$ stupid." The staff has made it clear that swearing is a point off the student's participation grade. The staff member nods and says, "I know it can be a frustrating exercise, but keep at it," addressing the student's apparent feelings rather than the comment. The student already knows that the comment was inappropriate and hurt his grade. The staff member didn't need to confront the student with the point violation at that time, as it may have only escalated the situation. Instead he chose to respond empathetically.

- A library aide is monitoring a group of students using library computers. The expectations are clear as to what students can and cannot use the computer for. She catches two students listening to an inappropriate song. She bans both students from the computer for the rest of the day and tomorrow.

Administrative Discipline: There comes a point when a behavior is severe enough that it needs a referral to the building administration. Most buildings have a clear policy on this. Behaviors like fighting, stealing, threatening, possessing drugs or alcohol, or bringing a weapon to school warrant notifying an administrator who can handle the situation. There are also times when students are so disruptive, defiant, aggressive, or emotionally escalated you will need to contact an administrator who can take more formal disciplinary action or steps to manage an escalating risk. If you face disciplinary problems regularly, it is important not to overuse your administration to solve problems. If you think you may need to make a referral to an administrator, it is best to discuss this option with the administrator beforehand.

- A paraprofessional in the library asks a student to stop talking. The student stands up and begins to swear loudly, berating her with a stream of obscenities. This causes a few other students to laugh. The paraprofessional refers both the student who swore at her *and* the students who laughed with a written disciplinary referral.
- A fourth-grade student has refused to do any work. When the paraprofessional encourages him to work he yells at her, stands up, and pushes her. She refers him to the principal's office for administrative discipline.

Your Personal Reaction

Students with behavioral issues often have a lot of difficulty handling conflict. An important concept to remember when working with these students is understanding how they perceive an argument. Their form of arguing has been called *process orientation*. Process orientation refers to the idea that these students are much more interested in the process of the argument than the outcome. That is to say, they care less about the consequences of their behavior during the argument or the outcome of the situation than about the argument itself. During an argument, the argument itself becomes their central focus. They will lose the war if they can win the battle. They will cut off their nose to spite their face. Most often, the way to "win" the argument is to control the mood of the perceived "opponent" (i.e., you).

Thus, your personal reactions while handling episodes of misbehavior are extremely important. Getting heated during an interaction with a student may be telling students they are "winning" or cause them to escalate the interaction. Unfortunately many people are not aware of their personal reactions. There are a lot of ways you might inadvertently show a student your frustrations through your verbal messages, facial expressions, or posture.

Verbal	Facial	Posture
• Raising your voice	• Grimacing	• Crossing your arms (defensive posture)
• Sighing loudly	• Making angry facial expressions	
• Breathing heavily		• Taking a challenging or towering posture
• Struggling with your word choice	• Looking defeated	
• Defending yourself or resorting to "comebacks"	• Appearing confused	• Getting too close to the student
• Stating that you are becoming irritated	• Staring down the student	
	• Rolling your eyes	

Avoiding a Power Struggle

There are two levels on which you can engage with a student: the content level (what is being talked about) and the process level (how the conversation is going). Students who want to frustrate staff members will often switch out of process and into content or change the content of the interaction to something completely different. This is not to say that every student who does this is deliberately trying to annoy you.

Watch how the staff member in this interaction is distracted by the process orientation.

> STAFF: "OK, Zach, it is time to clean up and get ready for seventh period."
> STUDENT: "I'm not done!"
> STAFF: "I understand, but you can finish this tomorrow."
> STUDENT (switches to process): "You are always picking on me; you never let me finish anything."
> STAFF: "No, I'm not; I am fair to all the students!"
> STUDENT (changes content): "Last week you let Eddie finish his work and you gave him five extra minutes."
> STAFF: "No, that is untrue! I only let him do that because…"

Can you see how this poor staff member is on the defensive, defending himself against imaginary accusations like a politician before an election? This interaction could go on forever. All that needs to happen is for the student to continue to accuse the staff member of different things and change the topic multiple times until fifteen minutes have gone by. Let's look at a different way the staff member could have handled this.

> STAFF: "OK, Zach, it is time to clean up and get ready for seventh period."

STUDENT: "I'm not done!"

STAFF: "I understand, but you can finish this tomorrow."

STUDENT: "You are always picking on me."

STAFF: "I know it's hard to put this away, but it is about time to go."

STUDENT: "Last week you let Eddie finish his work and you gave him ten extra minutes."

STAFF: "It sounds important for you to do this. I think you are doing a fantastic job on it, by the way. We will make sure you get to continue this later."

Frustration in Perspective

There are many sources of frustration when working with students. Below are some common sources I have collected from paraprofessionals:

- Feeling like the student is getting away with something
- Feeling controlled
- Feeling like you are not making a difference
- Feeling as though your attention has been "milked"

One of the biggest sources of frustration comes when you are working harder than the student is. In essence you are trying to do something that is beyond your control, like *make* them do their homework. In a *win-win* model, you are helping, not making, them be successful. When your classroom structure and behavior system put the responsibility on the student, your frustration for things that are not in your control should disappear.

Ben

I once consulted with a teacher who was very upset with a student named Ben. Ben absolutely refused to do his math in pencil. Each day he brought only pens to math, despite being told over and over that he needed to bring a pencil. The teacher, who grew more frustrated each day, began taking his pen away and giving him a pencil, only to find that he would quickly find another pen. When I met her I could tell this was frustrating to her. "How important is it that he write in pencil?" I asked. "It's not that important," she replied. "It is the principle of the whole thing." Together we came up with a plan: tomorrow she would announce to the class that math could now be done in pencil or pen; however, any math done in pen would be counted two points deducted from the final grade (2%). Now it was no longer oppositional to write in pen, it was simply dumb. The teacher didn't need to feel frustrated anymore because the student was empowered with the choice.

DE-ESCLATION AND CRISIS MANAGEMENT

There will be times when, despite all your preventive efforts, you will have to manage students who are emotionally escalated, explosive, and not thinking clearly. At such times, you will need solid, well-practiced, crisis management skills. Many students may say they are "in crisis" when they are upset. A true crisis involves a risk of danger. Often when a student reaches the point where they might hurt someone else, hurt themselves, or otherwise act unsafely they have lost the ability to think rationally. In these situations students will not be receptive to interventions, discipline or instruction until you are able to de-escalate them.

This section will cover verbal crisis management techniques. There are situations in which physical restraint procedures are needed to manage an unsafe situation. Restraints and other physical interventions should only be attempted by staff who are trained and currently certified. If you work in a setting where these procedures are necessary you should receive appropriate formal training. Physical intervention training is usually for staff who work in classrooms that serve special populations.

Crisis management is a complicated skill. It involves both understanding the principles of de-escalation and employing a strategy to resolve the crisis.

De-escalation Principles

The primary purpose of de-escalation is to negate the risk to others and to calm the escalated person. This must be done without giving in, escalating other students, or losing control of other students. In a crisis, safety is always the top priority. There are several important principles to keep in mind when managing a crisis.

1. *Follow Procedure*

Districts often have procedures for working with crisis situations. It is common for paraprofessionals assigned to work in an environment that serves disruptive students to be trained in a protocol for managing crises. If you are trained in this manner you should use this training instead of the procedures in this book. There are several reasons for this. First, following a procedure in a crisis helps all staff members work together more effectively. Second, using a technique you are trained in protects you and your district from liability.

2. *Avoid Escalating Responses.*

One of the most important aspects of crisis management is to avoid responding in a way that could further escalate the situation. In general, the less force you can use in a situation the better. By force, I am mainly talking about non-physical force. This includes your choice of words, tone, volume, and rate of speech. Using less force does not mean that you should use no force, but that the amount you use should never be more than required. Excessive force is likely to cause a rapid escalation. Physical touch of any kind, even if it is to guide a student should be avoided except where it is absolutely necessary to protect the safety of the student or others.

Potentially Escalating Responses:

- Getting too close to the student
- Repeating demands
- Acting disappointed in the student
- Touching the student
- Raising your voice
- Arguing
- Threatening discipline
- Grabbing something away from the student
- Confronting the student in the presence of peers

De-escalation Strategies

There are essentially two ways you can approach an escalating situation. First, you can delay intervention altogether if you think the problem can resolve without your help. Second, you can employ a de-escalation strategy.

Delay or Postpone Strategy

Why bother to engage with an escalated student if you think a few minutes stewing by himself will be sufficient to calm him down? Below are some ways a crisis might be avoided by postponement.

- Ask the student to take a break or time-out
- Separate students in conflict

- Postpone a conflict or discussion until the student is ready.
- Give the student plenty of space

De-Escalation Strategy

When de-escalating a student, you will want to have a plan to control the tenor of the situation. Going into the situation with a template of what you are going to say and do is very helpful. The following three step process gives you an idea of how this might be accomplished.

Step One: Manage Your Self: You are the most important element in a de-escalation intervention. It is thus critical that you do not approach the situation in an emotionally escalated state. The following are important to remember when employing a verbal de-escalation strategy.

1. *Slow it Down:* Remember that one of your core allies in de-escalation is time. In a crisis, sometimes people think they have to rush an upset person to calm down – but rushing someone is never calming. Time is your friend, so take every second. Take a deep breath, speak very slowly, and pause often. Slowing down will also help you stay calm.

2. *Keep appropriate distance:* People who are escalated hate to be crowded. Stand at least arms length away from them. This helps prevent them from feeling threatened.

3. *Short and Simple:* When engaging an escalated person use short, concise sentences. Their ability to process verbal information and complex messages will not be very good.

4. *Portray Confidence:* In a crisis, you want to be the person who displays confidence. Appearing strong, without appearing aggressive, is calming to students. Appearing weak, scared, anxious, or indecisive will engender similar feelings in them.

Step Two: Meet Students Where They Are: Your first contact with an escalated person should be to develop an alliance. The best way to do this is to meet the student where they are. Unfortunately, many people who intervene in a crisis begin intervening by challenging the behavior. Presenting yourself as someone who is going to contain or punish the behavior is likely to escalate the situation further. If a student is escalated and wants to fight, start by acknowledging that student's frustration. Do not start with your need for him to calm down. Escalated behavior usually occurs out of frustration. Addressing the underlying frustration is an important place to start the de-escalation process. Meeting students where they are means empathizing with their emotions even when you don't necessarily agree with the way they are acting them out.

Students may make many rash statements while in crisis. Try not to challenge things students say. For example, they may say that they are going to beat someone up or leave school. Do not argue with rash statements. Here are some things you can do that are effective:

1. *Ask Questions:* Asking clarifying questions of an escalated person can sometimes help them calm down, if you can do it before they are too angry. Avoid questions that are leading or rhetorical such as "what do you think you should have done differently?"

2. *Clarify and Repeat:* Once you understand what is going on, repeat it to the person so they understand that you understand if possible. Empathize with the student's feelings.

3. *Make Reassuring Statements:* Tell the student you are going to help them and invite them to work with you.

Step Three: Engage in Problem Solving: The important aspect of engaging in problem solving from a *crisis management* stand point, is not that you are going to resolve the problem – you may or you may not come to an acceptable solution. Engaging the student in a process at this point is important because it takes time and diverts the student away from acting rashly. It also helps the student think rationally by engaging the part of his brain used for reasoning. Engaging in critical thinking and dialogue is not possible when you are mad.

Do not solve the problem for the student. Instead, just spend a lot of time asking them what it is they want, why that is important, what they have done so far to try and make it happen, and how well it has worked. Really listen to the responses. Clarify what they say often.

Students sometimes make rash plans, especially at the beginning of problem solving. However, if in the end the student is still determined to harm himself or someone else, the issue will need to be referred to the teacher who may refer the student to an administrator, counselor, or school psychologist for a more formal assessment of risk.

Jon

Jill is a paraprofessional in a classroom for students with disruptive behaviors. A 5th grade student who is obviously very upset comes into class and begins throwing books off the shelf. Jill decides she should do something about this behavior quickly.

"Jon, I see you are throwing the books off the shelf, all over the place. What's going on?" Jill is calm and does not appear upset by the Jon's behavior.

"I hate this school, and I hate teachers, and I hate you," Jon yells in reply.

"Okay, I hear you," says Jill slowly. "You're really hating school right now, and all the teachers and me. Is that right?"

"Yes!" the student yells, kicking over an empty desk. Jill moves in closer, but not too close.

"Jon, I see whatever is going on has got you really frustrated. Is that right? I've never seen you this mad, I'm really concerned. Did something happen?" Jon

responds with a string of obscenities, heads to the back corner of the room and rips a poster off the wall.

"They got no right!" he yells, "No right to talk about me that way. Next time I hear anyone call me names on the playground, I'm going to get a knife and cut their head off." At this point Jon has said something pretty concerning. Jill could address the threat, but it would pull her calming strategy off course. She elects to handle it later.

"Whoa Jon. You seem pretty angry, back up a minute. Did someone call you a name just now? I really want to hear what is going on."

"Those kids on the playground, they said..." At this point, Jon begins to explain what happened. He describes how he is frequently teased at recess by many different students. Jill listens and nods her head. Not wanting to tower over him, she pulls up a chair and leans forward to listen. As Jon describes what is going on she listens to his voice and watches his body language. If talking about the situation and being listened to is calming for him, she keeps doing it. If telling her about the incident begins to rile him up too much, she is going to stop him. After a few minutes of listening, Jill decides she needs to stop him because he is working himself up.

"Gosh Jon, that sounds really terrible. I can see why you are so mad! And you know, I think that would make me mad too! It sounds like you are not being treated fairly at all and people are being unkind to you."

"Yeah," says Jon. He seems to settle down a little.

"Jon, can we sit down together. I want to find out more about this and you and I can try to stop this from happening to you again." Notice that Jill has still not mentioned any of Jon's inappropriate behavior yet. "Jon, what do you want to happen here?"

Jill and Jon discuss the matter with Jill setting a calm tone. She helps Jon generate some solutions of ways he can handle the problem next time. They decide that next time he is teased he will tell the playground assistant immediately. They rehearse the words he will say and Jill agrees to tell the playground assistant so she is prepared if the incident recurs. She helps Jon come up with some responses to the teasing. She also gets the names of the students that teased Jon today and agrees to talk to their teacher. The plan takes just five minutes to create, but by the end Jon is a lot calmer.

Now that the crisis part of the incident is over, Jill will follow up with the problem in several ways. First, the student created a significant disturbance. Once Jon is calm she might address the incident by asking him to repair any damage he created during non-class time. The threats Jon made to harm other students need to be examined in more detail, probably by an administrator or school psychologist. Jill refers the matter to the teacher who decides on the appropriate course of action.

DISABILITIES AND BEHAVIOR

If you work in the school system you will encounter many types of educational labels and diagnoses. It is important to understand what these types of labels mean—and what they do not mean. Some labels come from federal laws describing disabilities; some labels come from the mental health field. Frequently students with behavioral problems also have disability labels and/or diagnostic labels. This section attempts to shed some light on the more common terms you may see.

An important aspect of working with students with disability labels is to understand how that disability impacts them, what the label means, and how to make sure you work with the student appropriately. That means not giving a free pass to a student who has a condition by expecting nothing out of him, but it also means not punishing a student for a behavior she can't help. You wouldn't get angry with a deaf person for not hearing you. In the same way, it's not appropriate to get angry at a student with Asperger's syndrome for being overly rigid with his routines.

When it comes to more deliberate behaviors, the water gets muddier. What about a student who breaks the rules but qualifies for emotional disturbance because he has *Oppositional Defiant Disorder* (ODD)? In this case, we have a label that is descriptive of a behavior. That student is ODD precisely because he breaks rules. He does not break rules *because* he has ODD. We can expect that he is going to act contrary to the rules until he develops the skills to get his needs met in other ways. We aren't going to be surprised, when he acts consistent with his disability. We are going to provide ways to accommodate this kind of student so he still gets his education while building his skills and working on changing those behaviors that impact him.

Students with disabilities will have a plan that will provide *accommodations* (assistance meeting the expectations of the learning environment) and *modifications* (changes to the expectations). For students with disruptive behaviors, these plans are most often Individualized Education Plans (IEPs), or 504 plans. IEPs can make accommodations and modifications however 504 plans only involve accommodations. When you are working with a student with one of these plans, it is very important that you also work with the teacher and other staff to get to know and understand the specialized plans that have been developed. These plans are legally binding documents and are required to be followed under state and federal law.

Emotional Behavioral Disability (EBD): The term *Emotional Behavioral Disability* is an educational label. It is not, as it sounds to be, a psychological diagnosis. You may also hear this described as an *emotional disturbance (ED)* and students with his label are sometimes called *emotionally disturbed*. Students labeled EBD frequently (but not always) have behavioral difficulties.

A student with an Emotional Behavioral Disability has met certain criteria spelled out under federal law.

In general, these criteria say that the student has difficulty learning, maintaining satisfactory personal relationships, or managing emotions that adversely affect him or her at school. Obviously this definition can include some very different students; It might include a shy, depressed third grader who hides in the closet, or a boisterous, unruly ninth grader whose defiant behaviors cause daily disruptions, or an eleventh-grade boy experiencing a schizophrenic break. Students become eligible because the school feels they need specially designed instruction in one or more areas.

Emotional disturbance, as a label, says very little about a student or her capabilities, personality, or likely behaviors. All it means is there is an educational impact due to

FEDERAL CRITERIA FOR EMOTIONAL DISTURBANCE

Emotional disturbance is used to describe emotional and behavioral difficulties that require special education services. To qualify, students must exhibit one or more of the following characteristics over a long period of time to a marked degree that adversely affects educational performance:

- An inability to learn that cannot be explained by intellectual, sensory, or health factors

- An inability to build or maintain satisfactory interpersonal relationships with peers and teachers

- Inappropriate types of behavior and feelings under normal circumstances

- A general pervasive mood of unhappiness or depression

- A tendency to develop physical symptoms or fears associated with personal or school problems

Note that the term "EBD" includes schizophrenia but does not apply to students who are termed "socially maladjusted" Students who are substance abusers do not qualify as EBD unless they exhibit other behaviors consistent with the criteria.

an emotional issue. Often I have seen staff members raise an eyebrow when they hear a student who is "emotionally disturbed" will be coming to their classroom. This is unfortunate, as this label says very little about the student.

Learning Disability (LD): Students are classified as having *specific learning disabilities* when they have a disturbance in one or more of the basic processes involved in learning. Like an EBD student, an LD student has met certain conditions set forth by federal guidelines for identification. A learning disability involves an "imperfect ability to listen, think, speak, read, write, spell, or to do mathematical calculations" (IDEA, 2004) in a student with otherwise *normal* intelligence. Students with learning disabilities *can* learn; however, we often see them down on their abilities, believing they are "stupid." We commonly see much misbehavior from students with learning disabilities because they are frustrated with school. Helping a student with a learning disability often involves using alternative methods for instructing the student. When working with a student with a learning disability, make sure you know what is expected in terms of specific adjustments to his learning program.

Autistic Spectrum Disorders (ASD): Another disability category is the autistic spectrum disorders, or ASD. These include autism and Asperger's syndrome. Autism is defined as a developmental disability that has a significant impact on how the child communicates and interacts. Students with autism may engage in repetitive acts or movements, show a strong resistance to change or disruption in their environment or routines, and may have unusual sensory experiences. They may also have problems with fine and gross motor skills. Autism may, but does not always, impact intelligence. Because autism can be so different in so many different people, it is called a "spectrum" disorder, meaning that the degree of impact on individuals with autism can be a little or a lot.

Asperger's syndrome lies on the high functioning end of the spectrum. Many students with Asperger's syndrome will be indistinguishable from other students at first, but they manifest difficulties with social interaction, processing, sensory information (low tolerance for bright lights, large crowds, and loud noises), and have problems with transitions and changes in routine. Unlike other developmental disorders, students with Asperger's syndrome do not have significant delays in language or cognitive development.

Psychological Diagnoses

There are literally hundreds of different psychological diagnoses, but we will focus on a few that are fairly common in children in educational settings. A diagnosis does not define a child. In the mental health field we like to say the important question is not "What kind of diagnosis does the person have?" but instead "What kind of person has the diagnosis?" When we think about students this way, it helps us remember they are people and not labels.

Attention Deficit Hyperactivity Disorder (ADHD): ADHD is a very commonly diagnosed condition in students. It is classified in special education as "other health impaired" under IDEA. ADHD has some fairly general criteria, making it easy to diagnose and sometimes difficult to tell from other problems including anxiety, oppositionality and normal childhood boisterousness. The criteria include a problem with inattention. This might include difficulty sustaining attention to an assignment, organizing tasks and activities, and forgetting or losing school materials.

ADHD is not technically a deficit in paying attention; it is a deficit in filtering out unimportant sensory information. For instance, the student with ADHD will have a hard time concentrating and completing work in a noisy room because there are a lot of other things to attend to. ADHD doesn't mean a student can't focus. Some students even hyper-focus on an area of interest for some periods of time, tuning out even important things going on around them. Students with ADHD may also display hyperactivity—excessive energy such as running, fidgeting, etc., and impulsivity (blurting out answers, difficulty waiting his or her turn). The disorder is often treated with stimulant medications and in-school accommodations to the student's learning program.

Oppositional Defiant Disorder (ODD): ODD is a pattern of behavior characterized by opposition to authority figures. Students get this diagnosis because of their behavior. Many students with this diagnosis are choosing to engage in power struggles with adults. Other common behaviors associated with this diagnosis include refusing to comply with instructions, deliberately annoying others, blaming others for one's own mistakes. Students with ODD are also often spiteful and vindictive, easily annoyed.

Conduct Disorder (CD): Conduct Disorder is a more serious form of behavior disorder in that the behaviors of this disorder include major violations such as aggression, property damage, theft, or other serious rule violations. Students with conduct disorder have sometimes been called *socially maladjusted,* although the two terms are not synonymous. Despite the seriousness of the behavior associated with this disorder, it is specifically excluded from qualifying as a disability under IDEA. Many see students with conduct disorder as performing deliberate behaviors that do not stem from an emotional difficulty for this reason, many students with serious behavior who do not qualify for special education wind up expelled or in alternative programs because of their behavior. Often students with conduct disorder may have other mental health conditions that allow them to qualify under IDEA as emotionally disturbed.

Bipolar Disorder (BPD): Bipolar disorder has only recently begun to be assigned as a diagnosis in children. This disorder used to be called *manic depression.* In adults the disorder manifests in distinct periods of manic and depressed activity lasting for days or weeks at a time. Children cycle through manic and depressive stages much more rapidly, such that distinct periods of mania or depression at not discernible. Bipolar disorder in children is often characterized by extended rages, excessive energy, strong reactions to limit setting, and frequent mood swings without perceptible triggers. Bipolar disorder can be hard to diagnose, as many of these symptoms can also occur in children with other disorders such as ODD or ADHD.

Anxiety Disorders: Anxiety disorders are a class of psychological disturbance in which the dominant features are fears and worries. These include generalized anxiety disorder, specific fears (phobias), panic attacks, social phobias, obsessive-compulsive disorder, and many others. Anxiety is a common feature among students experiencing difficulties. Often the escape and anxiety-management strategies a student uses may manifest as behavior. Students with anxiety may avoid school, work, or social situations, and act out when confronted.

Post-Traumatic Stress Disorder (PTSD): PTSD is an anxiety disorder that arises because a student has experienced or witnessed a severely traumatic event and has a difficult time handling the associated emotions. Some common events that trigger PTSD include child abuse, sexual abuse, and witnessing violence. Children who witness trauma in their developing years may also have trouble regulating emotions, controlling impulses, and solving problems.

Tourette's Syndrome: Tourette's syndrome is a disorder that often includes motor and vocal tics. A tic is an involuntary movement or vocalization. Tics might include eye blinking, twirling, grunting, coughing, grimacing, hand flapping, tongue protrusions, and sniffing, just to name a few. An uncommon but well known tic, *coprolalia*, involves uttering obscenities. Obsessions and compulsions, hyperactivity, and impulsivity are often associated with Tourette's syndrome. Many students with Tourette's also endure social shame from their involuntary behaviors.

Depressive Disorders: There are many different varieties of depression. These may include a major depressive disorder with severe disturbance in mood or a long-standing, low-grade depression (i.e., dysthymia). Symptoms of depression can include not only outward signs of sadness, such as crying or reporting sad feelings, but may also include poor appetite, difficulty sleeping, low energy, low self-esteem, poor concentration, diminished interest in pleasure, agitation, and aggression. Students with depression often present cognitive distortions such as seeing the world, their future, and themselves through a very negative lens. Suicidal ideation is often a concern with depressed students. Below are some warning signs of suicide. If you have any concerns about a student, it is essential you bring them to someone trained to intervene, such as a counselor or school psychologist.

Warning Signs of Suicide
- Talk, thoughts, or drawings with death/suicide as the theme.
- Signs of clinical depression including loss of appetite, sadness, irritability or loss of interest in activities
- Giving away favored possessions, saying goodbye, tying up loose ends
- Sudden improvement in mood (often people's mood improves after they decide to commit suicide)
- Acquiring means to harm oneself (e.g. weapons, pills)
- Other self-harm behaviors indicative of extreme personal pain (i.e. cutting)
- Risk taking behavior (e.g. driving fast)

Will Henson is a graduate of the California School of Professional Psychology at Alliant University in San Francisco CA. Dr. Henson works as a special education consultant to programs that serve students with emotional and behavioral disorders. Dr. Henson consults on issues of program development, staff training, and risk management. He also provides clinical services which include case consultation, psychological evaluation and risk assessment. Dr. Henson and his family live in the Portland OR metro area.

Made in the USA
Lexington, KY
08 December 2010